PUPPET BOX

is crammed with lots of ideas for making your own puppets, from the simplest finger puppets to a complete traditional Punch and Judy. There are instructions for shadow puppets, marionettes, felt puppets, a ventriloquist's dummy, as well as puppets you can make out of corks, wooden spoons – even old socks! Discover how to put on a show, from writing a script to using special effects – it's all in PUPPET BOX!

CW00840517

Also available in Knight Books:

PAPER BOX
Juliet Bawden

HOW TO HALT A HICCUP AND OTHER HANDY HINTS
Mary Danby

THE RAINY DAY SURVIVAL BOOK
Jeremy Tapscott

DIRTY, LOUD AND BRILLIANT
Carol Vorderman

PUPPET BOX

JULIET BAWDEN

ILLUSTRATED BY MANDY JOHNS

KNIGHT
BOOKS

HODDER AND STOUGHTON

Copyright © 1990 by Albury
Technical Services

First published in Great Britain in
1991 by Knight Books

**British Library Cataloguing in
Publication Data**
Bawden, Juliet
Puppet box
1. Puppets, Making
I. Title. II. Johns, Mandy
745.59224

ISBN 0 340 53231 9

Printed and bound in Great Britain
for Hodder and Stoughton Children's
Books, a division of Hodder and
Stoughton Ltd., Mill Road, Dunton
Green, Sevenoaks, Kent TN13 2YA.
(Editorial Office: 47 Bedford Square,
London WC1B 3DP) by Cox & Wyman
Ltd., Reading, Berks.

For Katherine, Edward and Anthony with love

CONTENTS

INTRODUCTION

Puppets can be made from almost anything and that includes household rubbish, old cardboard boxes, tin cans, wood, sticks, scraps of fabric, balls of wool and papier mâché.

Puppets work in one of two ways, either being moved from above like string puppets or from below like glove or rod puppets.

This book gives you a little of the history of puppets and shows you how to make various kinds including finger, glove, shadow and string. It shows you how to make a theatre and put on a show.

There are very simple projects and some which are quite difficult. There are projects costing next to nothing and other which cost a little more.

The list of tools and materials is quite long but you won't need all of them for each project. Every project has a list of tools and materials at the top so you can just collect together the things needed for any particular project. And remember, always take care when using craft knives or scissors, and always ask permission before cutting up old clothes, magazines, etc – somebody might want them!

Have fun!

TOOLS AND MATERIALS

TOOLS

- cotton thread
- pins and needles
- wools
- buttons
- pencils
- felt tips
- paints
- glue
- ruler or tape measure
- string
- wire
- tin snips (for cutting wire)
- shirring elastic
- paper
- tracing paper
- bucket
- water
- wallpaper paste
- foam
- scissors
- screen and projector

MATERIALS

You can make puppets from almost anything, so it is a good idea to collect things as they turn up. Next time your mum is about to throw out an old cereal carton, keep it and use the cardboard. Tubes are very useful for arms and legs, so keep the insides of loo rolls and kitchen foil, paper etc. You will have to buy some new things and these are listed on the next page. You will also need to collect scraps of fabric and wool to make bodies and hair.

OLD MATERIALS

Get a big box to store all your large pieces of "rubbish" and collect the following:

- newspaper
- empty cardboard containers, including tissue boxes, cereal and washing powder boxes, match and toothpaste boxes and egg boxes
- lolly sticks
- yoghurt cartons and old paper or wax paper cups
- old socks, gloves and mittens (these can be used for glove puppets)
- old vests (for faces)
- paper bags
- old envelopes
- cotton reels
- corrugated cardboard
- brown wrapping paper
- postcards

Get a small shoe box or something similar to collect small bits and pieces, and anything that is pretty and may be used as part of a costume or figure, including:

- elastic bands
- buttons
- sequins
- scraps of fabric
- ribbon
- tin foil
- old wrapping paper or stickers
- old tights

NEW MATERIALS

You will probably have to buy some new materials. Some of these items can be purchased in haberdashery departments in large shops. Other things may be bought in specialist craft or stationery shops.

- pipe cleaners
- fabric pens
- stuffing
- felt in lots of colours
- plastic doll and teddy noses and eyes
- fake fur fabric

HELPFUL HINTS ON PUPPET MAKING

Most of the puppets in this book you can make by just tracing off the pattern or by following the instructions. However, a few of the puppets have to be made from a pattern that may need enlarging.

ENLARGING A PATTERN

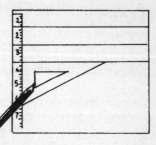

1 Take one of the patterns in the book and on a large piece of paper draw the same number of squares as are on the pattern but to a larger scale. You will need a set square, ruler and a pencil. Start at the top left hand corner of the page and draw vertical lines evenly spaced down the page. Then draw the horizontal lines, using the set square to make sure that the lines are at right angles. (As an alternative you can use dressmaker's grid paper.)

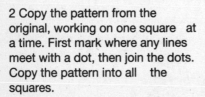

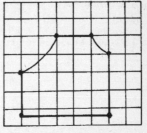

2 Copy the pattern from the original, working on one square at a time. First mark where any lines meet with a dot, then join the dots. Copy the pattern into all the squares.

3 Add seam allowance to the outside of your pattern. Use the pattern to cut out your puppet.

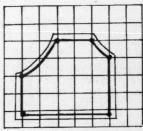

TRACING PATTERNS

Some patterns you will need to trace.

YOU WILL NEED

● tracing paper
● masking tape
● medium hard pencil, such as an HB
● scissors
● pins

INSTRUCTIONS

1 Place the tracing paper over the pattern. Hold it in place by means of masking tape.

2 Go over the image with a pencil.

3 Remove the masking tape, lift up the pattern and cut out the shape.

4 Pin the shape on to your fabric, and cut round it to make the puppet.

CUTTING OUT A PATTERN

Cutting out a pattern is quite easy but many puppets go wrong at this early stage of making, so bear the following advice in mind.

1 Make sure that you have all the pattern pieces you need to make your puppet.

2 Make sure that you have enough material. To do this, arrange the pattern pieces on the material and make sure that they fit. You may be using different kinds of material, in which case, fit each pattern piece on to its respective fabric. Try and arrange the pieces so that you waste as little material as possible.

3 Check whether the pattern requires you to cut one or two of any pattern, then make sure that you cut the correct number of pieces.

4 Pin all pieces before cutting so that you cut them accurately.

STICKING BITS TOGETHER

Glueing things together should be easy, but it can be very messy. Below are some guidelines.

1 It is important to use the correct kind of glue for the job you are doing. As a rule you will need plastic glues for plastic components and animal glues for fabrics. However, if you are in doubt check the label and follow the instructions carefully.

2 Don't use too much glue; it usually goes further than you think. If you are having to dispense glue from a jar, use a tool for spreading the glue – an old emery board is good for this or a lolly stick.

3 Try not to glue too large an area at one time, as it will be very soggy and probably takes ages to dry. When glueing a large area, press from the middle outwards so that the glue can spread evenly and to push away any air bubbles.

4 When glueing something tiny like a finger puppet, mark the seam allowance with a biro and only put the glue up to the biro line. This will help prevent you sticking the whole front of the puppet to the back.

5 Wait for the glue to dry properly before you start using the puppet or you will be disappointed with the results.

SEWING PUPPETS

If you don't stick your puppets you may need to sew them. Some puppets, such as finger puppets, need so little sewing that it is quite easy to do. Running stitches and back stitches are the best for sewing simple seams.

For large glove puppets and clothes for puppets you usually sew the front to the back with the insides facing each other, so that when you turn the puppet or clothes the right way round the seams are hidden.

For finger puppets the seams are so narrow and the puppets so tiny it is better to leave the seam on the outside.

Here are a few simple rules to help you.

1 Choose a thread to match your fabric. It will be less noticable than a contrasting thread and if your stitching isn't brilliant it won't show up too much.

2 Pin the pieces together before you start so that they don't move around whilst you sew.

3 Always start your sewing with a knot and end by oversewing so that the seam does not come undone.

4 Don't forget to remove all the pins before using the puppet!

THE HISTORY OF PUPPETS

Puppets have been in use all over the world from very early times. Many famous writers, such as Shakespeare, Voltaire, Plato, Byron and Goethe have used puppets to illustrate their work. But where did puppets come from originally?

This is one legend which gives an answer. Once upon a time there was a poor carpenter who lived in an Indian village. The other villagers were also poor and often he had very little work to do. So he used to carve dolls for his neighbour's children. One day Siva, the god of music, was passing through the village with his wife. The goddess saw the carpenter and was so impressed with the carved dolls she said to Siva, "They are so lifelike! What a pity they cannot move. Shall we breathe life into them?"

Siva agreed and in no time at all the dolls sprang to life and began to dance around and sing. The carpenter was overjoyed, but only for a short time. Siva and his wife went on their way, and as they did so the spell was broken and the dolls slumped to the floor lifeless once again. The carpenter ran after Siva and his wife imploring them to return. Siva replied "Honest carpenter the dolls are yours. You made them, it is up to you to find a way of bringing them to life."

The carpenter walked back to his shop a sad and bitter man. He sat and thought of ways in which he might bring the dolls to life. After a long time he decided to tie string on the ends of their fingers and toes. The carved dolls became puppets and from then on the carpenter could make them sing and dance as much as he wished.

Moving statues are mentioned at the birthday celebration of Osiris, in ancient Egyptian literature. The ancient Greeks appear to have used puppets: a golden statue of Apollo is said to have moved itself by springs. At Preneste the statue of Juno and Jupiter as children sitting on the knee of Fortune is said to have moved.

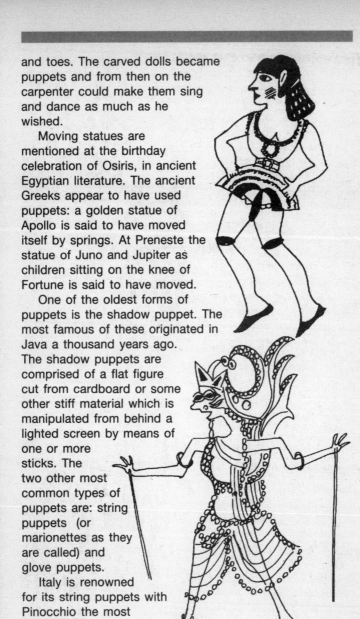

One of the oldest forms of puppets is the shadow puppet. The most famous of these originated in Java a thousand years ago. The shadow puppets are comprised of a flat figure cut from cardboard or some other stiff material which is manipulated from behind a lighted screen by means of one or more sticks. The two other most common types of puppets are: string puppets (or marionettes as they are called) and glove puppets.

Italy is renowned for its string puppets with Pinocchio the most famous.

England is particularly known for Punch and Judy, although Punch originated in Italy as a character called Pulcinella, a hunchback with a hooked nose, who was always in trouble! Other European countries have their own versions of Punch: in France he is "Polichinelle", in Germany he is "Kasperle" and in Russia he is "Petrouchka".

Puppets can be any size you want, from tiny to giant, such as the ones used for carnival. Religious and popular processions were an opportunity to use large puppets. Each country or region would depict its mythical heroes and antiheroes. For example a large puppet dragon in Paris would be slain by St Michael and the people would throw money, sweets, cakes and flowers in the path of these giant puppets. Often puppets were used to enact mystery plays in cathedral squares or at fairs. In Paris during the seventeenth century there was a famous puppet-eering family called Brioche, who incidentally also practised dentistry. They presented puppets at the French court and from that moment puppets became popular entertainment in the drawing rooms of the well-to-do.

In 1784 a pleasure centre was built for the people of Paris. Part of the attraction was Brioche and his "Theatre of Pygmees".

Puppets were not only being developed in Europe. The Japanese marionette theatre is one of the most exceptional in the world. Many of the puppets are life-sized and some need two or three people to operate them.

SHADOW PUPPETS

Shadow puppets are thought to have originated in China, moved on to Asia and then to Malaysia, Indonesia, Turkey and Greece. They were particularly popular in Europe during the eighteenth and nineteenth centuries. Lit from behind, shadows would be projected on to a screen. The puppets themselves were made out of cardboard which was moved on rods.

On the following pages we give you some ideas to make shadows using only your hands as the puppets.

YOU WILL NEED

- a source of light (either a candle or a lamp without a shade)
- a screen or a blank wall

INSTRUCTIONS

1 Put the light in front of the screen or wall.

2 Put your hands between the light and the screen.

3 Imitate the shapes which the hands on the following pages are making.

4 Get a friend to do the same, so that you create a play, for example a dog chasing a rabbit.

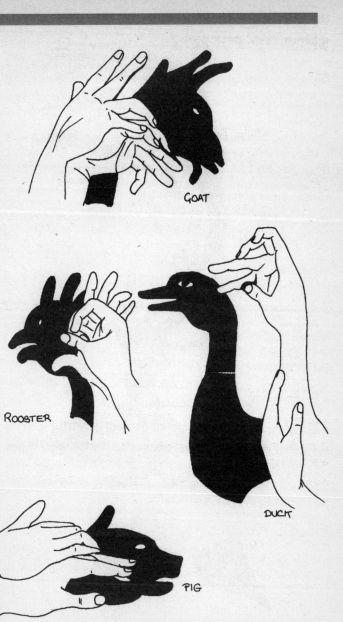

GOAT

ROOSTER

DUCK

PIG

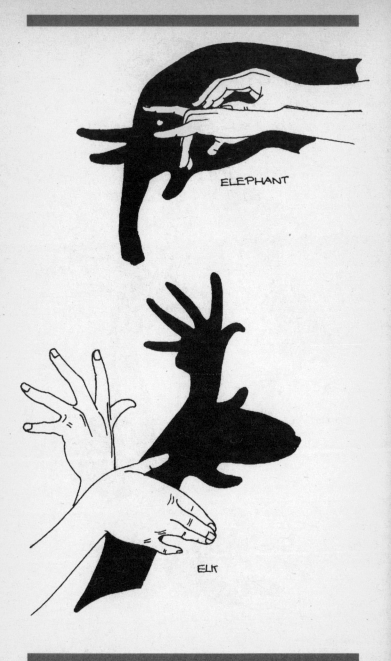

ELEPHANT

ELK

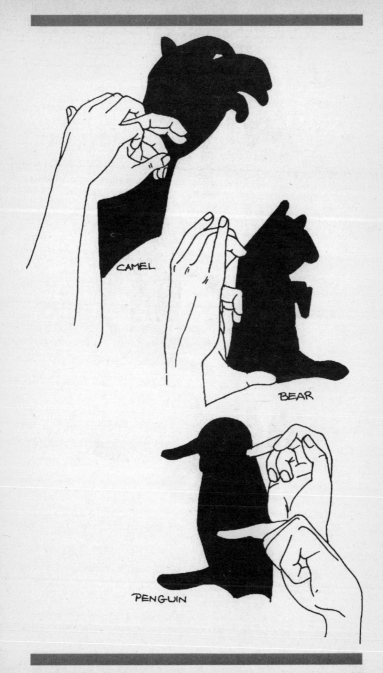

CAMEL

BEAR

PENGUIN

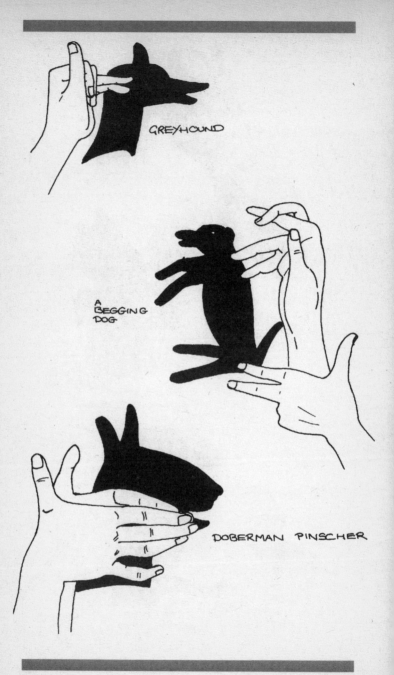

GREYHOUND

A BEGGING DOG

DOBERMAN PINSCHER

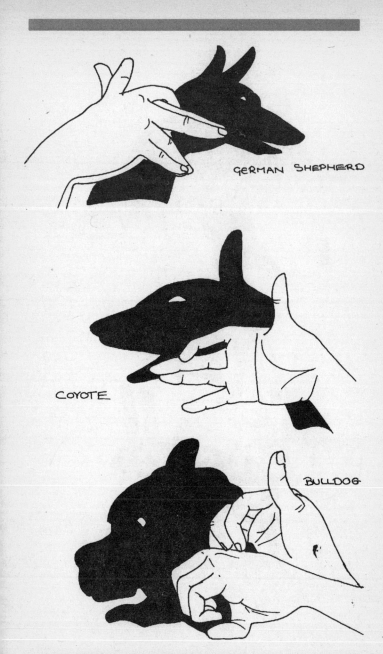

GERMAN SHEPHERD

COYOTE

BULLDOG

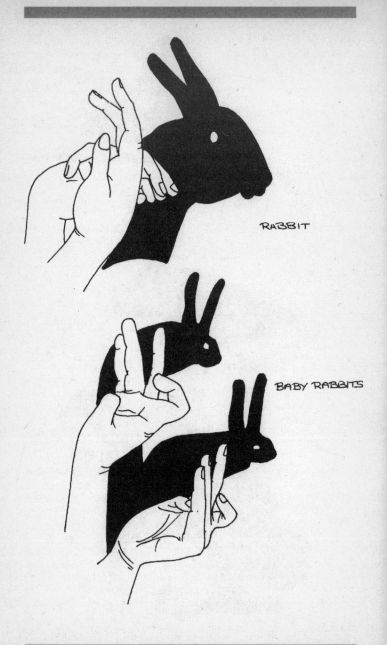

RABBIT

BABY RABBITS

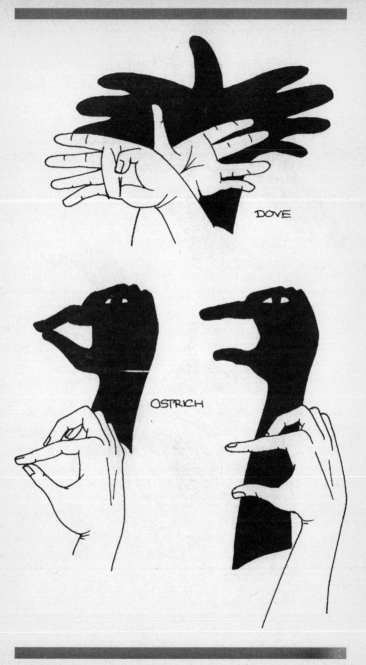

DOVE

OSTRICH

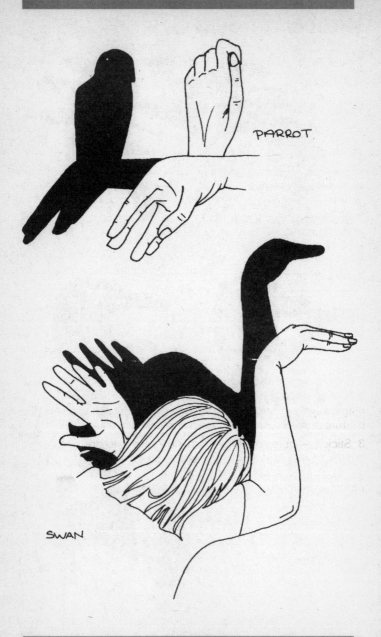

PARROT

SWAN

SHADOW CUT OUTS

These are very easy to make and can look very effective.

YOU WILL NEED

- old magazines
- cardboard (old cereal packets will do)
- black poster paint or watercolour
- glue and sticky tape
- lolly sticks (optional)
- scissors
- cardboard box
- white tissue paper
- lamp
- skewer

INSTRUCTIONS

1 Paint the cardboard black and leave it to dry.

2 Cut out figures, leaving a 1cm ($^3/_8$ in) border around each figure, from the magazines (fig 1). Try to choose figures in different poses, a mixture of men, women, children and animals.

3 Stick the figures on to the card (fig 2), leave to dry, and cut out the figures without the border this time.

4 Glue or tape the stick or a cardboard strip on to the shape (fig 3) so that you can move it.

2.   3.

5 To make the stage, cut the front and back off the box.

6 With a skewer make a series of holes all over the base of the cardboard box. These are to stand your puppets in. You may have to enlarge these holes for the lolly sticks to fit – adjust as necessary.

7 Stick a tissue paper screen on to the back of the box. If you want scenery, stick twigs or leaves or even a New York skyline on to the tissue paper.

TO PUT ON THE SHOW

1 Stand the box between two chairs, so that the bottom of the box is over a gap and you can move the stick puppets. Secure with tape on to the chairs.

2 Set up the light behind the screen; remember to keep out of the way as you move your characters around as you don't want your shadow interfering with the play!

3 Gather your audience together and turn off the main lights, turn on the stage light and start to work.

BRAINWAVES

Make shadow puppets work on a piece of paper which slots into the side of the box and is pulled backwards and forwards to make it appear as if the figures are moving. Swing characters from above. Or make a revolving stage.

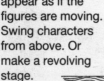

PUTTING ON A SHADOW SHOW

Once you have perfected hand shadows and cut outs, you may want to do something more daring. Because shadows are always flat you can do unusual things behind a screen. For example in the picture below a surgeon is taking a variety of unusual objects from his victim's stomach!

You can add cardboard props to your body to change your whole profile, so you can look as though you have a hump back, a tail, a large nose or even rabbit ears. The method is the same as just using your hands to project a shadow but instead you use the whole of your body!

REAL FINGER PUPPETS

Most people think of puppets made from felt when you mention finger puppets, and they normally think of face painting when painting any part of the body. Well, below we have a combination of fingers and body painting to produce real finger puppets!

You can paint the whole hand to create characters or paint the fingers as individual people or animals. You can add props. A ribbon round the wrist can be a bow for a cat and a circle of paper can be a hat on top of a finger character.

YOU WILL NEED

- ball point pens
- felt tips
- crayons
- powder paint and water
- paper and pencil

INSTRUCTIONS

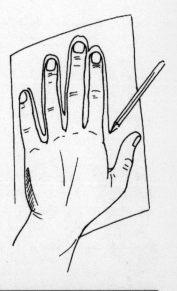

1 Draw round your own hand on to a piece of paper and use this paper hand to design on.

2 Wash and dry your hands so they are clean.

3 As your skin will absorb colours it is a good idea to paint it white to start with, so that the colours will stand out.

4 Paint or draw the outline first and then fill in with colours.

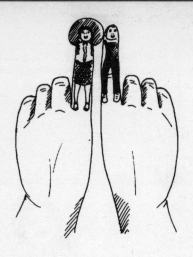

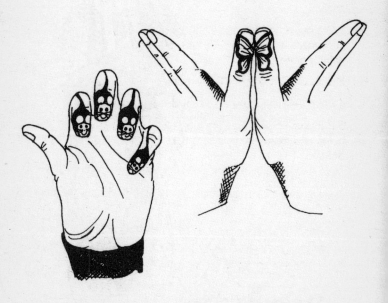

HOLE IN CARD PUPPETS

These puppets use your fingers as part of the puppet and a piece of card as the rest. Sometimes your finger will be a nose, sometimes legs and sometimes a tongue. Some of the puppets involve cutting one hole and sometimes two.

YOU WILL NEED

● tracing paper and pencil
● cardboard (cereal packets or tissue boxes will do)
● scissors
● paint and a brush

INSTRUCTIONS

1 Trace out one of the patterns on to the card.

2 Cut out round the edge and then, if the cardboard is grey, give it a coat of white paint. Leave it to dry.

3 Cut out the holes for the fingers.

4 Paint the design on to the card.

5 Put your fingers through the holes and make the puppet dance.

Dancing Lady

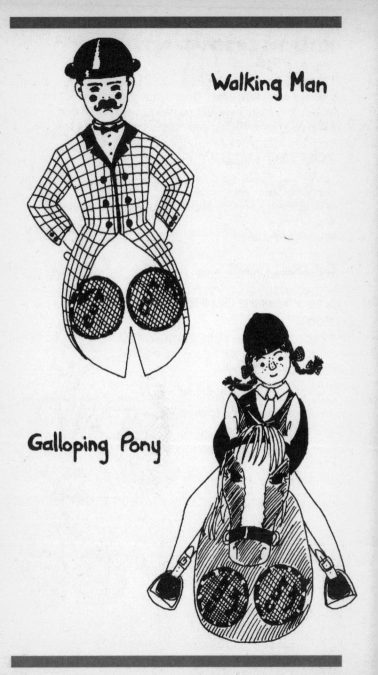

Walking Man

Galloping Pony

Humpty Dumpty

This elephant and the clown on the next page only have holes for one finger. For the elephant, paint your finger grey to make his trunk, and for the rude clown, paint it pink to make his tongue.

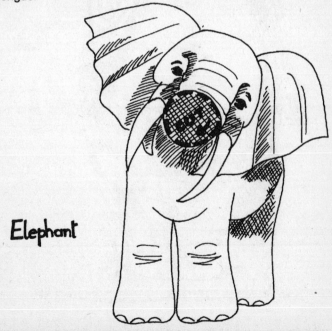

Elephant

Rude Clown

WOODEN SPOON FAMILY

This is an easy way of making puppets.

YOU WILL NEED

- three wooden spoons, 1 large, 1 medium and 1 small
- felt tips
- scraps of wool
- scissors
- glue stick
- paper
- fabric and oddments, of ribbon
- needle and thread
- paper doily

INSTRUCTIONS

1 Turn the back of the spoon so it is facing you. On the large spoon draw a man's face with a moustache and a monocle (fig 1).

2 On the middle-sized spoon draw a woman's face. Cut some strands of wool for hair and stick them into place (fig 2).

3 On the small-sized spoon draw a baby face (fig 3).

4 For the daddy spoon, cut a collar and tie shape from paper, colour them in and stick into place (fig 4).

5 Cut a piece of material approximately 25cms (10 in) wide and 10cm (4 in) deep and sew a line of running stitches along one of the long sides.

6 Gather up the running stitches and wrap the material around the handle of the mummy spoon (fig 5). Put some glue on the handle to help stick this in place.

7 If the gathers look ugly, tie a piece of ribbon round the spoon to cover them (fig 6).

8 For the baby spoon, cut out the centre of the doily. Gather the outside frilly bit into folds and stick it in position (fig 7).

9 Draw shoes and socks on all the puppets.

5.

6.

7.

WALKING FINGER PUPPETS

These puppets can be good fun especially if you use pictures of friends and give them inappropriate bodies!

YOU WILL NEED

- old magazine or photo of a friend or relative
- scissors
- thin card
- glue
- paints and a paint brush
- piece of paper

INSTRUCTIONS

1 Cut out the head from the photograph or magazine and stick it on to card, leaving enough room to draw the body. Draw a funny body shape on to the card.

2 Cut out the head and body together. Decorate the body.

3 Bend the feet forward so they stand flat.

4 Cut two pieces of paper, each about 2.5cm (1in wide) and roll them into tubes to fit your fingers. Glue them so that they won't unroll.

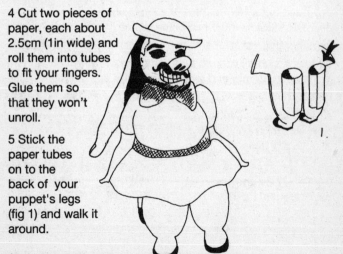

5 Stick the paper tubes on to the back of your puppet's legs (fig 1) and walk it around.

MOP PUPPET

This puppet uses a mop as a head of hair.

YOU WILL NEED

- scissors
- sponge ball
- mop
- bits of felt
- glue
- piece of fabric
- needle and thread
- pipe cleaner
- felt tips

INSTRUCTIONS

1 With the scissors, make a hole down the centre of the sponge ball and push the ball up the mop so it is just below the mop head hair (fig 1).

2 Cut out bits of felt to make the eyes, nose and mouth. Stick them into place on the sponge head to make a face.

3 Make a skirt as you did for the mummy in the spoon family and wrap it round the handle.

4 Make arms by wrapping a pipe cleaner around the handle and twisting it into position.

5 Paint shoes and socks on the bottom of handle.

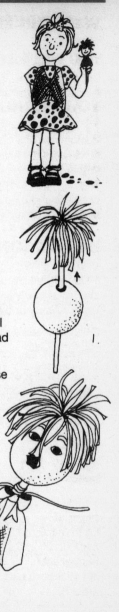

SPIDER PUPPET

YOU WILL NEED

- one section of an old carton egg box
- paint and a paint brush
- 2 red sequins, stickers or pieces of felt
- glue
- 8 green pipe cleaners
- masking tape
- black shirring elastic and a needle

INSTRUCTIONS

1 Paint the egg box black, and either stick or paint on red eyes and sharp white teeth.

2 To make the legs, wrap the pipe cleaners around each other and stick them to the underside of the egg box.

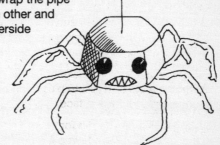

3 Thread the shirring elastic on to the needle, knot the end and thread through the centre of the egg carton.

4 Bounce the spider up and down to frighten your friends.

UNDERSIDE

DISCO DANCER

YOU WILL NEED

- ping pong ball
- scissors
- paper napkin
- piece of thread
- sequins and glue
- felt tips
- pipe cleaner
- paper
- rubber band

INSTRUCTIONS

1 Make a hole in the ping pong ball about 25mm ($^1/_{10}$ in) wide

2 Unfold the napkin and then pick it up by its centre and twist it into a point. Insert the point into the hole in the ping pong ball.

3 Tie a piece of thread round the centre of the napkin and spread out the bottom half to form the skirt.

4 Decorate the skirt with felt tips and sequins.

5 Twist the pipe cleaner round the body to make the arms.

6 Draw the dancer's face on the ping pong ball.

7 Make shoes for her out of two cones of paper, twisted round to fit your first and second fingers. Stick them into position.

8 Decorate the cones so they look like shoes.

9 Attach the dancer to your wrist by means of a rubber band.

CORK FINGER PUPPETS

Corks make very good tops for finger puppets, especially champagne corks which are wider at the top.

YOU WILL NEED

- corks
- scissors
- paper or thin card
- glue
- felt tips
- bits of wool or raffia

INSTRUCTIONS

1 Cut a piece of paper or card wide enough to go round the cork with a slight overlap.

2 Stick this piece of paper on to the cork about halfway down.

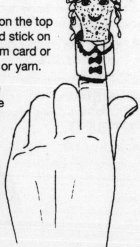

3 Draw a face on the top of the cork and stick on a hat made from card or hair from wool or yarn.

4 Decorate the cardboard tube and the rest of the cork to make a body.

5 Push your finger into the cardboard tube to work the puppet.

POM POM PUPPETS

From one pom pom pattern you can make
a variety of animal puppets

YOU WILL NEED

- 2 pieces of card, 20cm (8 in) square
- a plate
- pencil
- scissors
- jam jar or lid, 5cm (2 in) across
- 225gm (8oz) wool in one or various colours
optional
- scraps of felt
- fabric glue
- pipe cleaners
- shirring elastic
- sequins

INSTRUCTIONS FOR BASIC POM POM

1 Using a plate draw a circle approximately 20cm (8 in) in
diameter, on both pieces of card.Cut out both the circles.

2 In the centre of each circle, make another circle of about
5cm (2 in) in diameter. This can be done by drawing round a
jam jar or lid. Cut out both circles.

3 Put one piece of card on top of the other and tie them
together, wind the wool round and round until all
the card is covered (fig 1).

1.

4 Carefully cut round the edge with the scissors, keeping one blade between the pieces of card (fig 2).

5 Pull the pieces apart. Tie a piece of wool very tightly around the centre of the ball (fig 3).

6 Remove the card and fluff out the woollen ball.

SPIDER

1 Make the pom pom from black wool.

2 Add black pipe cleaner legs twisted round each other and through the centre of the pom pom to hold them in place.

3 Stick on two red sequin eyes.

4 Suspend from black shirring elastic.

EASTER CHICK

1 Make 2 yellow pom poms, one slightly larger than the other and tie them together.

2 Cut a yellow diamond shape from felt. Fold it in half and stick in place for a beak

3 Make 2 yellow legs from pipe cleaners.

ROBIN

As for the Easter chick, but using brown and red wool.

SNAKE OR CATERPILLAR

Join together lots of pom poms.

SOCK PUPPETS

This is something to do with all those odd socks which seem to be in most people's homes!

YOU WILL NEED

- an odd sock
- felt tip
- bits of felt
- buttons
- fabric glue

optional
- pipecleaners
- sequins
- needle and thread

GREY SEAL

The simplest puppet to make is a seal; you will need a grey sock, two black button eyes and three white pipe cleaners.

INSTRUCTIONS

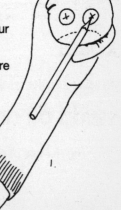

1 Put the sock on your hand, with your fingers where the toes should be and your thumb where the heel should be.

2 Bend your hand slightly and mark where the eyes and the nose should go (fig 1).

3 Stick on the black buttons for eyes.

4 Cut a felt nose and stick this in position.

5 Thread the pipecleaners through the end of the sock under the nose to make the whiskers (fig 2).

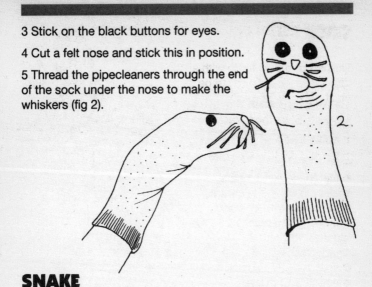

SNAKE

Use a multicoloured sock or stick on lots of coloured felt patterns.

Follow steps 1 and 2 as for the seal.

3 Cut a forked tounge from felt and stick or sew into position.

4 Decorate the body by sticking on brightly coloured bits of felt and buttons, sequins etc.

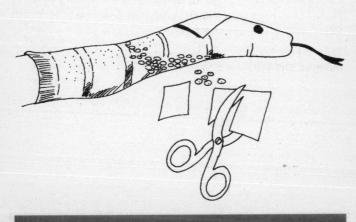

CAT

Steps 1 and 2 as for the seal.

3 Cut diamond shaped eyes from yellow or green felt with black centres. Stick them into position.

4 Make a pink triangular felt nose and stick into position.

5 Cut triangular felt ears, make a pleat in the centre and then sew them on to the sock. Add pipe cleaner whiskers.

DRAGON PUPPET

This puppet uses up old postcards and greetings cards.

YOU WILL NEED

- old postcards and greetings cards
- scissors
- hole punch
- green and red paint
- brush
- 2 milk bottle tops
- glue
- drinking straws
- thin string
- 2 pieces of dowelling

INSTRUCTIONS

1 Cut one of the greetings card into an oval shape (fig 1). Punch or cut a hole in the centre and fold the oval in half.

2 From one of the cards cut a tongue shape (fig 2).

3 Cut a tail shape from another piece of card (fig 3).

4 Paint the face green, the tongue and tail red.

5 Stick bottle top eyes on to the face (fig 4).

6 Punch or cut a hole in the centre of each card.

7 Cut the straws in half.

8 Thread the cards on to the straws (fig 5).

9 Tie one end of the tongue on to the string, and through the hole in the dragon head (fig 6).

10 Pass the string through all the straws with cards on them.

11 Tie the other end of the thread on to the tail.

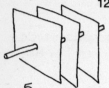

5.

12 Tie a long piece of string on to each piece of dowelling and then tie each to a piece of string between two straws on the puppet (fig 7).

13 Work the puppet by moving the dowelling up and down.

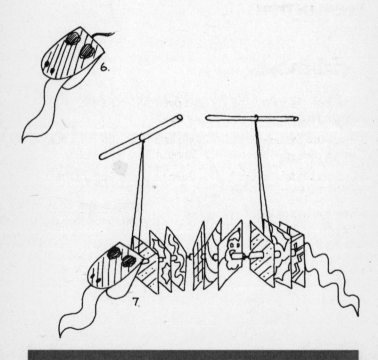

6.

7.

HAND PUPPETS

From this one pattern you can make lots of different kinds of puppets by changing the colours of the felt used and the features that you stick on.

Depending on which character or animal you are making , trace and cut out the features from the pattern given.

YOU WILL NEED

- tracing paper and pencil
- 1 piece of felt 42cm (17 in) x 20cm (8 in) in a suitable colour for your puppet: green for a frog, golden yellow for a lion, grey for a monkey, etc.
- scissors
- fragments of felt in other colours
- fabric glue
- needle and thread

INSTRUCTIONS

1 Trace off the pattern on the next page and cut it out, enlarging it if necessary to fit your hand.

2 Place the pattern on folded fabric as shown and cut it out. This will give you two pieces of fabric, a front and a back.

3 Cut out the features and stick them on to the front of the puppet. Leave them to dry.

4 Sew the two sides of the puppet together, using a very small seam allowance.

BRAINWAVES

Make pirates, clowns, ducks and sheep, all by this method.

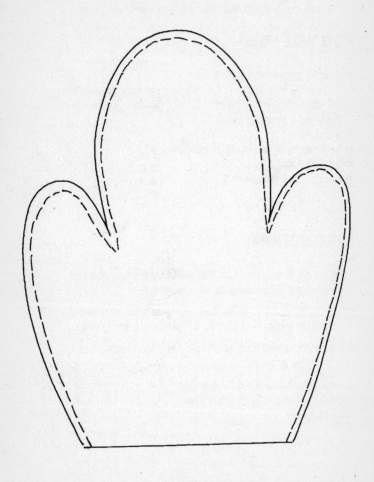

FELT FINGER PUPPETS

Finger puppets are fiddly to make but are very cheap as they don't use much fabric.

You can make all kinds of creatures and characters from the one basic pattern by adding variations in the way of sequins and buttons, bits of wool, etc.

YOU WILL NEED

- tracing paper and pencil
- scissors
- felt in various colours
- dressmaker's pins
- fabric scraps
- fabric glue
- needle and thread

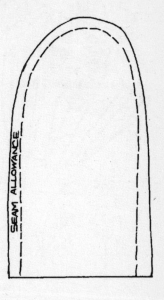

INSTRUCTIONS

1 Trace off this pattern and cut it out.

2 Fold a piece of felt in half and pin the pattern on to it.

3 Cut out the felt and remove the pins and pattern.

4 Stick the features on to the front of the finger puppet. Leave them to dry.

5 With a running stitch, sew the puppet front to the back.

BRAINWAVES

Make characters from nursery rhyme stories, for example
Goldilocks and the three bears. Make a complete zoo or
Noah's ark pairs of animals.

Or make finger puppets with arms; these are a little more
difficult to make but are more interesting to look at.

FINGER PUPPETS WITH ARMS

YOU WILL NEED

- tracing paper and pencil
- scissors
- felt
- dressmaker's pins
- fabric scraps
- fabric glue
- needle and
  thread
- small amount
  of wadding or
  old tights for
  stuffing.

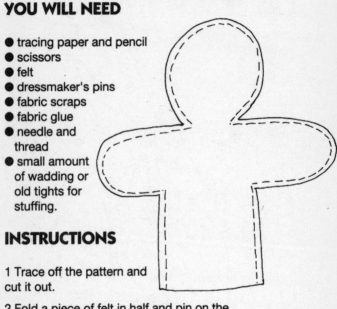

INSTRUCTIONS

1 Trace off the pattern and
cut it out.

2 Fold a piece of felt in half and pin on the
pattern piece.

3 Cut out the pattern in felt and remove the pins and pattern
piece.

4 Stick the features on the front of the body shape and then leave them to dry.

5 Pin the front to the back of the puppet and tack and then sew them together (fig 1)

6 Carefully push tiny amounts of stuffing into the arm and head spaces to make them look padded (fig 2).

7 Sew the stuffing into position (fig 3).

PAPIER MÂCHÉ FINGER PUPPETS

These are easy finger puppets to make and are very effective.

YOU WILL NEED

- cardboard (e.g. old cereal packet)
- scissors
- masking tape
- newspaper
- wallpaper paste
- paints and paintbrush
- varnish

INSTRUCTIONS

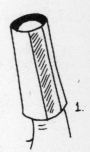

1 Cut a strip of card about the same height as from the top of your finger to just past the second joint, and wide enough to wrap round your finger with an overlap.

2 Wrap the card round your finger, adjust it to fit and then stick the side with masking tape (fig 1).

3 Stick a wodge of newspaper on to the end of the tube and hold it in place with masking tape (fig 2).

4 Cut a circle of cardboard to fit as a hat over the top of the tube.

5 Cut lines radiating from the centre of the circle and stick this over the top of the puppet (figs 3 and 4).

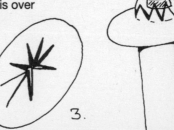

6 Make papier mâché by dipping newspaper strips in the wallpaper paste, removing the excess glue and covering the outside of all the card with the gluey paper (fig 5).

7 When the puppet, including the hat, has been completely covered, leave it to dry. Do another two coats of papier mâché as you did the first. Leave to dry between coats.

8 Paint a face and clothes on the puppet (fig 6), and when it is dry varnish it.

BRAINWAVE

Make other characters, so you can have a complete story on one set of fingers.

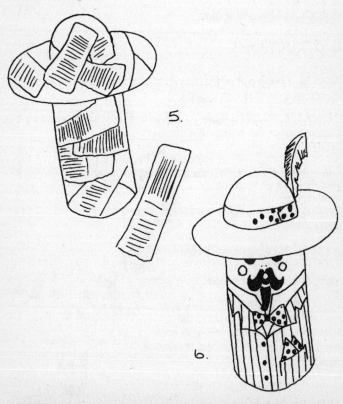

5.

6.

PAPIER MÂCHÉ HEAD PUPPET

YOU WILL NEED

- Plasticine
- empty lemonade bottle
- Vaseline or soap
- wallpaper paste
- newspaper
- craft knife
- masking tape
- 2 sticks or 2 plastic straws
- paint and brush
- wool for hair
- cloth, needle and thread

INSTRUCTIONS

1 Model a head out of Plasticine. (If you are making lots of characters do them all together.)

2 Stick the modelled head on top of the lemonade bottle (cut the bottom of the bottle off first).

3 Cover the head completely in Vaseline or soap. This will stop the Plasticine sticking to the papier mâché.

4 Mix up the wallpaper paste according to the instructions on the packet.

5 Rip the newspaper into strips about 1cm (³⁄₈ in) wide and dip them one by one into the glue and then stick them all over the Plasticine head.

6 When the head is completely covered in paper strips leave it to dry. An airing cupboard is a good place for this.

7 When the head is dry cover it with more strips of paper to form another layer. Leave this layer to dry.

8 Repeat steps 6 and 7 a few more times until you have between six to eight layers.

9 When all the layers are dry, using a craft knife cut the head in two very carefully as you want to keep both pieces.

10 Remove the Plasticine head and stick the papier mâché head together with masking tape back on to the bottle neck, if you have had to take it off when removing the Plasticine.

11 Cover the neck and joins with another layer of papier mâché. Leave this to dry and repeat with one more layer of papier mâché.

12 Pierce a hole in the lemonade bottle near the top. Push the straws, dowelling or sticks through the holes to make arms.

13 If you want fat arms and hands, add papier mâché to the arms in the way you did to the head. Leave to dry.

14 Paint the head and arms white, then when they dry paint them flesh coloured.

15 Paint features on the face and add hair, if it is a human puppet. For an animal add the animal markings and features.

16 To make the costume, cut a rectangle of cloth with a hole in the centre big enough to fit over the puppet's head. The cloth should be wide enough to cover from one arm to the other and twice as long as the body of the puppet (the lemonade bottle).

17 Put the cloth over the head of the puppet and then make it fit round the neck by sewing with a few running stitches round the neck hole and drawing them up tight round the neck.

18 Sew up the sides of the rectangle.

19 Fit your hand in the puppet to make it work.

SNAPPING DRAGON

It is nice to be able to make something from rubbish that would otherwise be thrown away, so keep boxes, cartons, lemonade bottles, etc, to make puppets.

YOU WILL NEED

- 2 egg boxes
- scissors
- masking tape
- paint and brush
- an old sleeve from a cardigan
- fabric glue
- 2 milk bottle tops
- bits of felt in orange and green

INSTRUCTIONS

1 If the egg box is hinged along its length, cut it along the join and rejoin it along its width, using masking tape (fig 1).

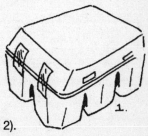

2 Paint the inside of the box green.

3 Insert the box into the sleeve. Cut down the side of the sleeve so that the box will open like a jaw (fig 2).

4 Glue the raw edges of the sleeve to stop them fraying.

5 Cut 2 egg containers from the other egg box and paint them red.

6 Wash the milk bottle tops and stick those on top of the egg containers (fig 3).

7 Stick these on top of the sleeve near the hinge to make the eyes (fig 4).

8 Cut out flame shaped pieces of red and green felt and stick them down the length of the arm.

9 Make a tongue from felt and stick it in the centre of the egg box (fig 5).

10 Put your hand in the sleeve and grasp the box, snap it open and shut.

ROD PUPPET

YOU WILL NEED

- old sock or pair of tights
- cotton wool or old tights or socks for stuffing
- stick (this could be an old spoon)
- string
- bits of fabric for sticking on features
- scissors
- fabric glue
- fabric felt tips
- wool
- rectangle of material
- needle and thread

INSTRUCTIONS

1 Stuff the sock with cotton wool or socks to make the head.

2 Push the stick or spoon head first up into its centre and secure with some string.

3 Cut out features from scraps of fabric and stick them into place on the sock face, or draw in features with a felt tip pen.

4 Stick on bits of wool for hair.

5 Cut a rectangle of material and do a line of running stitches along one long side.

6 Gather up the running stitches around the neck of the stick and secure with a knot.

7 Decorate the skirt with more bits of fabric, lace or felt tip pens.

DISH CLOTH PUPPET

YOU WILL NEED

- newspaper
- old dish cloth or J-cloth cut in two or an old handkerchief
- string
- paint and a paint brush

INSTRUCTIONS

1 Screw the paper up into a round ball.

2 Wrap the cloth round it and then tie it at the neck with a longish piece of string, so that the head is secure and you also have a loose end of about 25cm (10 in) long.

3 Arrange the folds of the cloth so that the front is smooth to form a face. Paint on face.

4 Make arms by twisting the cloth on either side of the head and tieing string around these, again leaving 25cm (10in) long ends.

5 Make a loop on the end of each piece of string to work the puppet.

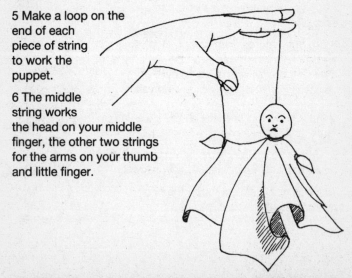

6 The middle string works the head on your middle finger, the other two strings for the arms on your thumb and little finger.

PUNCH AND JUDY

YOU WILL NEED

- paper, pencil, ruler and set square
- cardboard tubes from the centres of kitchen rolls
- large and small scissors
- flesh coloured foam in both 5mm (¼ in) and 2.5cm (1 in) thicknesses
- fabric glue
- red and pink felt tip pens
- red, white and blue felt
- 1 ball each of yellow and white wool
- 50cm (20 in) of 40cm (16 in) wide fabric in white, cut into a circle
- needle and thread
- 50cm (20 in) of 1.5cm (⅝ in) wide lace
- 75cm (30 in) of 90 cm (36 in) wide fabric in red and 40cm (16 in) of 90cm (36 in) wide fabric in blue
- 3.6m of yellow ric-rac
- 70cm (28 in) of 1.5cm (1⅝ in) braid
- 4 buttons
- 50cm (20 in) of 2cm (¾ in) wide white ribbon
- 70cm (28 in) of 5cm (2 in) wide yellow ribbon

TO MAKE PATTERNS

Square up patterns by the method shown on p13. One square is equal to 2.5cm (1 in). The patterns include 5mm (¼ in) seam allowance. All seams are sewn with right sides together; the pieces are then turned inside out so that the seams are hidden inside.

CUTTING OUT

PUNCH

From fabric:

A glove or body – cut 2 in red
B hat – cut 2 in red.

From felt:

B lips – cut 1 in red
C outer eye – cut 2 in blue
D middle eye – cut 2 in white
E inner eye – cut 2 in blue

From foam:

A hand – cut 2 from thin foam
B ear – cut 2 from thin foam
C cheek – cut 2 from thick foam
D nose – cut 1 from thick foam
E chin – cut 1 from thick foam

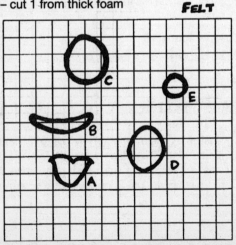

FABRIC

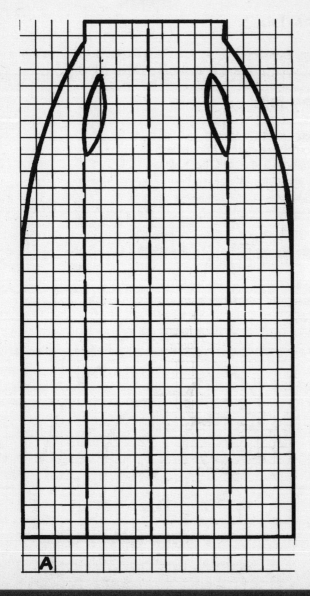

A

JUDY

From fabric:

A glove or body – cut 2 from blue fabric. Cut a circle with a 40cm (16 inches) diameter from white fabric

From felt:

A lips – cut 1 from red
C outer eye – cut 2 from blue
D middle eye – cut 2 from white
E inner eye – cut 2 from blue

FABRIC

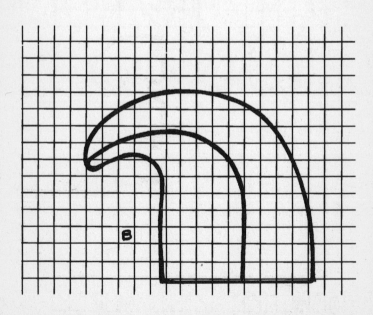

From foam:

A hand – cut 2 from thin foam
B ear – cut 2 from thin foam
C cheek – cut 2 from thick foam
F nose – cut 1 from thick foam
G chin – cut 1 from thick foam

FOAM

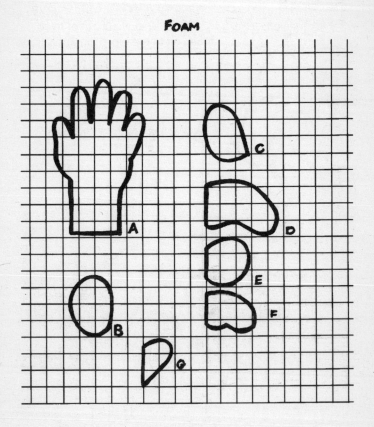

INSTRUCTIONS

HEADS

1 Cut the cardboard tube so it is 18cm (7^1/$_2$ in) long for Judy and 23cm (9^1/$_4$ in) long for Punch.

2 Wrap thin foam round both tubes and glue into place. Trim off any excess foam and make sure the join line is at the back (figs 1 and 2).

3 Stick the nose, cheeks and chin, already cut out of thick foam, on to the tubes (fig 3).

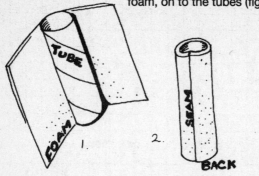

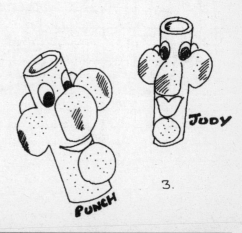

4 Use felt tips to colour the end of the nose and the cheeks.

5 Stick the felt eyes and mouth into place on the foam face (fig 3).

6 Stick the ears to the sides of the head behind the cheeks. In the case of Judy's ears, make a small tuck in them to make them stick out.

HAIR

1 For Punch, cut white wool into 10cm (4 in) lengths and stick these from just in front of the ears working round to the back of the head, level with the top of the tube head.
For Judy, cut 18cm (7¼ in) lengths of yellow wool and stick as you did for Punch (fig 4).

4.

HATS

For Judy

1 Neaten the edge of the white circle with a row of running stitches.

2 Sew another circle of thread 3cm (1¼ in) in from the edge of the circle and pull up so that the hat will fit over the top of the head (fig 5).

3 Fill the hat with a few foam scraps to bulk it out. Fit it on the head and make sure the ends of the sewing thread are secured with a knot or back stitch.

For Punch

1 Attach ric-rac where the dotted lines are marked on the hat pattern.

2 Sew the two hat pieces together along the curved edges with the right sides, which have the ric-rac on them, on the inside and then turn through to right way round.

3 Sew ric-rac along seam lines.

4 Make a tassel from wool and attach to the end of the hat.

5 Stuff the hat with foam leftovers. Attach the hat to the top of the head.

6 Cut a hat band 12.5cm (5 in) x 6.5cm (2¾ in) from red fabric. Sew on 2 lines of ric-rac.

7 Stitch the two ends of the hat band together to form a tube and make a narrow hem along the top and bottom edge.

8 Slip hat band over the hat and glue into place.

Punch's body

1 In one piece of glove pattern cut 2 holes for the arms.

2 Stick ric-rac along the outside dotted lines.

3 Stick braid down the centre of one of the body pieces.

4 Sew on buttons at equal intervals down the braid.

5 Sew the two pieces of the glove pattern together, with right sides inside, along the long sides, then turn through to the right way round.

6 Cut 2 pieces of red fabric 15cm (6 in) x 6.5cm (2¾ in) and neaten one long side with running stitches. Attach ric-rac 3cm (1¼ in) from the neatened edge.

7 Join the short sides to form a tube and sew the un-neatened ends into the holes for the sleeves.

8 Make small tucks in the wrists of the foam hands and sew them into the ends of the sleeves.

For Judy – make as for Punch but omit the ric-rac

JOINING BODIES TO HEADS

1 Sew a line of running stitches round the neck of the body. Slip body over the head. Draw up the running stitches and stick into place.

2 Gather up the yellow ribbon along one edge and secure into place for Punch to make a collar.

3 Add a lace trim to Judy's neck.

OPTIONAL

Make a frilly white apron from white fabric with a lace trim and white ribbon.

POP UP PUPPET

This is another puppet made from things you can find around the house.

YOU WILL NEED

- old tights
- scissors
- cotton wool (or more old tights)
- rubber band
- empty yoghurt pot or cottage cheese carton
- a stick 40cm long (16 in)
- thread
- glue
- ribbon
- felt or other bits of material
- poster paints and brush
- wool or wool fringing

INSTRUCTIONS

1 Cut one of the feet off the tights including a 30cm (12 in) length (fig 1).

2 Stuff the foot end with tights or cotton wool to make a head. Put the rubber band round the head to hold in the stuffing (fig 2).

3 Make a hole in the bottom of the yoghurt pot big enough to take the stick. You may need to start the hole with a skewer or a pair of scissors.

4 Push one end of the stick through the yoghurt pot and the other end into the head of the tights (fig 3).

5 Push the yoghurt pot up to meet the tights and then tie the open edge of the tights to the mouth of the yoghurt pot. Stick into place as well to secure (fig 4).

6 Tie a piece of ribbon over this join to hide it.

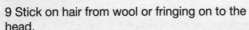

7 Cut facial features and hands from felt and other bits of fabric and stick them on to the head and body. (fig5)

8 Decorate the pot with poster paints to make it look pretty.

9 Stick on hair from wool or fringing on to the head.

10 Make the puppet appear and disappear by pushing and pulling the stick.

BUTTON PRINCESS

From a few old buttons and left over balls of yarn you can make unusual puppets. They move by thread which passes up and down the button holes!

YOU WILL NEED

- a small ball of white yarn (for her head)
- 1 skein of wool in red, yellow or black for her hair (tapestry wool comes in skeins)
- 1 skein of wool for her arms
- 18 small round beads
- 9 big buttons (for her body, neck and feet)
- 1 small button (for the top of her head)
- 2 needles and thread
- 2 lolly sticks crossed in the middle and glued

INSTRUCTIONS

1 Thread each needle so it has a double thread with a knot in the end.

2 Make a small loop in one end of the thread. Thread the needle down through one of the holes in the foot button, up through another one and then through the loop. (This sounds complicated but if you follow fig 1 you will get it right.)

1.

3 Now make the rest of the princess by threading up one leg 9 little beads.

4 Now pass the thread through 1 hole on each of 6 buttons for the body starting with the biggest at the bottom.

5 Plait the arm skein of wool and make a knot in either end of the skein. Pass the thread through the skein (fig 2).

6 Pass the thread through the big neck button and then through the ball of yarn for the head and the twisted skein of wool for the hair.

7 Follow steps 2-6 (but using the same plait for the arms and the same body and neck buttons) to make the other side of the body.

8 When you reach the top, thread both needles through a small button on the top of the head, pull the threads tightly and knot them together.

9 To make the princess move, attach threads to the ends of each arm, and to the top of her head. Attach these to the lolly sticks to move them.

2.

BRAINWAVES

Make other puppets such as a prince or a dog by the same method but add different details. Use pipe cleaners for arms and a moustache.

NEWBORN BABY

This baby is cheap to make as he is mainly old tights or stockings. It has a wonderful scrumpled face like most newborn babies.

YOU WILL NEED

- leg from a pair of flesh coloured tights
- stuffing, such as polyester
- 40cm (16 in) square of fluffy fabric
- small piece of lace or ribbon
- darning needle and thread
- dressmaker's pins
- glue or sticky tape

INSTRUCTIONS

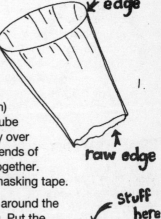

1 Cut a 25cm (10 in) long piece from the leg of the tights and half fold it inside out to make a 12.5cm (5 in) tube of double fabric (fig 1).

2 Cut a 5cm (2 in) x 12.5cm (10 in) piece of card and bend it into a tube that will fit easily and comfortably over your forefinger. Glue or tape the ends of the cardboard to hold the tube together. Cover one end of the tube with masking tape.

3 Make a line of running stitches around the raw edge of your folded stocking. Put the cardboard tube inside the stocking tube and draw the stitches up so that they fit comfortably round one end of the cardboard tube, then glue the two together at the bottom (fig 2).

4 Sew a line of running stitches along the other, folded end of the stocking tube. Fill the stocking with stuffing (fig 3) and then gather the stitches up tightly.

5 Pull the gathers in the top of the head down, so that the head is tight with stuffing, to the stitches at the bottom of the tube. Sew the bit you have pulled down to the neck of the tube to hold it in place (fig 4).

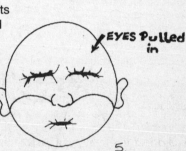

Pull over

3.

4.

6 Start making the features, by sewing from the back of the head to the front using a double thread in the same colour as the tights. The thread will crease and pull the tights giving the face a scrunched appearance (fig 5).

7 Cut the body from the Mr Punch pattern (p73) and add the sleeves in the same way.

EYES Pulled in

5.

9 Gather the body on to the baby's head (babies don't have much neck at this age). Add a ribbon or broderie anglaise frill to cover the neck join (fig 6).

10 Make a hand by cutting a piece of tights 15cm (6 in) long and double it as you did for the head.

11 Gather the raw edges, turn the other way round and fill with stuffing. Gather the other end, then pull the two lots of gathers together and sew so they are joined. Stitch the fingers as you did the features for the face (fig 7).

6.

12 Make a second hand as you did the first.

13 Sew the hands into the gathered up ends of the sleeves.

BRAINWAVES

Make a gruesome granny or grandad in the same way but with lots of vertical lines around the mouth and the middle 0f the forehead to mark ageing.

Stitches

7.

TUBE PUPPETS

To make this puppet you will need a cardboard tube with a circumference large enough to fit your hand and arm inside.

YOU WILL NEED

- cardboard tube
- scissors
- masking tape
- a large potato
- tin foil
- crepe paper
- glue
- matchsticks
- two toothpaste tube tops
- egg box

1.

INSTRUCTIONS

1 If the tube is very long, cut it to fit your arm. Stick the potato on to the top of the tube using masking tape (fig 1).

2 Cover the potato in the tin foil and secure this with masking tape (fig 2).

2.

3 Cut a long piece of crepe paper and frill or serate the edges (fig 3).

3.

4 Starting at just under the neck stick the crepe paper to the tube and then spiral it down to cover the tube (fig 4).

5 Stick on matchstick hair through the foil and into the potato. Make eyes from the tops of the two toothpaste tubes, and a nose from one section of an egg box (fig 5).

BRAINWAVE

Stick on dried pasta for hair.

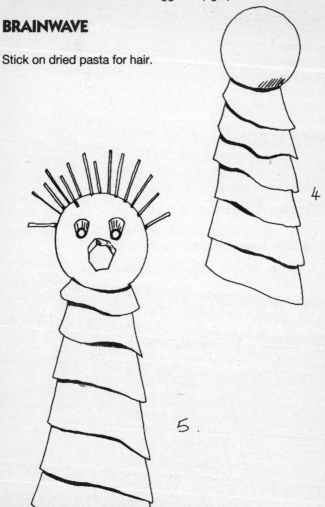

4.

5.

OCTOPUSSY

YOU WILL NEED

- circle of bubble wrap about the size of a dinner plate.
- old tennis ball
- elastic band
- scissors
- shirring elastic
- needle and thread
- 2 lollipop sticks
- black Fablon

INSTRUCTIONS

1 Wrap the bubble wrap around the tennis ball and secure with an elastic band (fig 1).

2 With scissors cut 8 legs (fig 2).

3 Cut 9 pieces of shirring elastic and attach them to the eight legs and the head of the octopussy.

4 Tie the two lolly sticks together to make a cross.

5 Attach the other ends of the elastic to the lolly sticks .

6 Cut out eyes and mouth from black Fablon and stick into place.

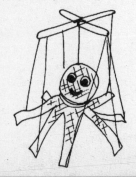

LANKY LEAN MONKEY

YOU WILL NEED

- newspaper or a roll of wallpaper
- sticky tape
- a friend
- biro
- paper, pencil, ruler and set square
- scissors
- large cardboard boxes or pieces of card
- brass paper fasteners
- paint and brush
- string
- stick or piece of dowelling
- a stool to stand on

INSTRUCTIONS

1 Either stick sheets of newspaper together or lay out the wallpaper plainest side up.

2 Lay your friend on the paper and draw round him or her; this is to help you work out the size of the legs, feet, torso, etc for your puppet.

3 Size up the pattern (see p13) then cut out pattern shapes for all the body pieces and the head from the newspaper or wallpaper. Use these to draw round on to the card to make your puppet.

4 Cut out the head and body shape from card and then copy the face below to make a monkey.

5 Joint the limbs by pushing the brass fasteners through the card where indicated and then opening them out on the back.

6 Paint the body and face.

7 Attach string to the fingers, elbows and knees, and then tie the string to a stick or a piece of dowelling. Stand on a stool and use the strings to manipulate the puppet.

FASTENERS

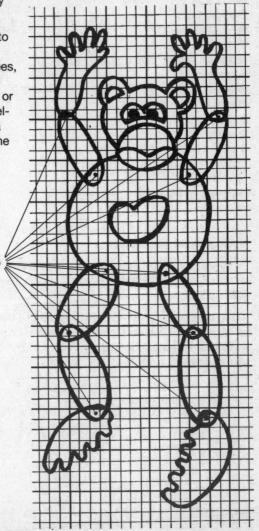

POTATO HEAD PUPPET

YOU WILL NEED

- potato
- apple corer
- 2 drawing pins
- 2 coins
- felt tip
- J-cloth
- scissors
- 2 rubber bands

INSTRUCTIONS

1 Clean and scrub the potato.

2 Remove a section of the potato from its centre using the corer. This is for you to put your finger in.

Drawing Pins

Coins

3 Stick 2 drawing pins in the front of the potato for eyes and 2 coins in the sides of the potato for ears.

4 Draw a nose and mouth using the felt tips.

5 Cut a hole, just large enough to insert your finger through, in the centre of the J-cloth.

6 Push your forefinger through the hole. Put the potato head on top and then get a friend to secure two ends of the cloth over your thumb and little finger using elastic bands.

PAPER BAG PUPPET

YOU WILL NEED

- paper bag
- glue stick
- scissors
- coloured felt tips

INSTRUCTIONS

1 Fold the bottom corners of the paper bag back and stick them into position (fig 1).

2 Cut two holes near to the bottom of the bag and just large enough for your fingers.

3 Decorate the bag with a charactoer. For example a witch, chef, clown or astronaut.

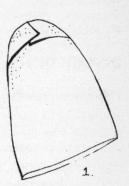

1.

TO WORK

Put your hand in the bag and use your forefinger to make the head wiggle about. Put your thumb and second fingers through the holes and use them as the puppet's arms. Tuck the other fingers into the bag.

JUMPING JACK

YOU WILL NEED

- paper, pencil, tracing paper
- card
- scissors
- felt tips or paints and brush
- knitting needle
- darning needle
- brass paper fasteners
- strong thread
- thin cord
- bead

INSTRUCTIONS

1 Draw the figure you wish to make on to paper (fig 1).

2 Trace off the limbs and torso individually on to card (fig 2) and cut the pieces out.

3 Decorate each piece of card, painting on the features and the costume.

4 Using the knitting needle pierce holes in the pattern pieces (marked on fig 2).

5 With a darning needle, make smaller holes (marked on fig 2) not too near to the edge on each of the limbs.

1.

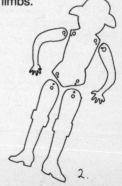

2.

6 Lay the limbs on the back of the body and from the front push the brass paper fasteners through the larger holes and open them out at the back.

7 Push the darning needle with thread through the smaller holes and join the arms together and the legs together.

8 Tie the thicker cord to the centre of the leg and arms thread. Put a bead on the bottom and use this to pull – the arms and legs will jump up and down.

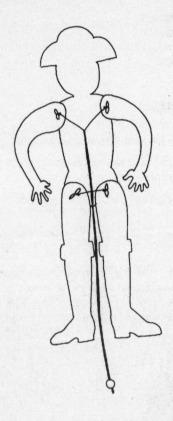

CUDDLY MONKEY

This monkey is lovely and he will cling
on to you like a real pet.

YOU WILL NEED

- 1 square metre (3 square feet) of fun fur fabric
- scissors
- ruler or tape measure
- needle and thread
- 23cm (9 in) square of felt in pink, red, brown and grey
- 10cm (4 in) of velcro
- toy animal eyes

INSTRUCTIONS

1 Cut 2 pieces of fur fabric 50cm long and 12cm (20 x 4³/₄ in)
wide. This is for the body.

2 Cut 2 pieces of fur fabric 56cm x 10cm (22¹/₂ x 4 in) for the
legs.

3 Cut 2 pieces of fur fabric 52cm x 10cm (20³/₄ x 4 in) for the
arms.

4 Cut 1 piece of fur fabric 29cm x 5cm (11¹/₂ x 2 in) for the tail.

5 Shape one end of each of the two body pieces into an oval
shape (fig 1).

6 Cut out a pink oval of felt 10cm (4 in) long and 15cm (6 in)
wide. Shape the ends so it will fit into the curved end you just
cut.

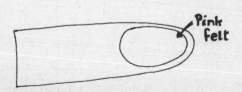

Pink
felt

1.

7 With the right sides of the body facing each other insert the mouth piece.

8 Sew one half to the top piece of fur and the other to the bottom piece (fig 2).

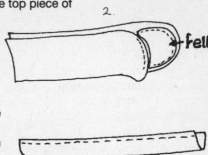

2.

←Felt

9 Sew the limbs by folding them in half (wrong side out) and sewing the two long edges together (fig 3). Turn right side out.

3.

10 Cut 8 pieces of grey felt each 7cm x 5cm (2¾ x 2 in) Sew two pieces on to one end of each limb, enclosing the raw edges of each (fig 4).

4.

11 Sew the arms in 20cms (8 inches) down the side seams (fig 5) and the legs at the bottom of the back of the body.

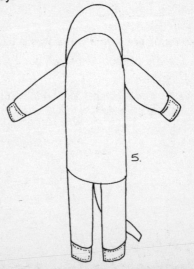

5.

12 Sew the tail (wrong side out) down the long sides as you did the arms. Turn it right way round and sew it in the centre of the back piece.

13 With right sides facing, sew the front to the back at the side seams. Turn right way out.

14 From felt, cut monkey features (fig 6) and stick or sew them on to the front of the monkey.

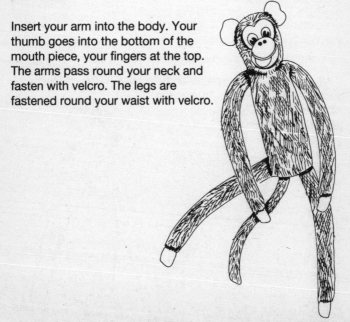

15 Cut ears and eyes (or use toy animal eyes) and add these on to the monkey. Make a red tongue and insert into the mouth piece.

16 Stick or sew velcro on to the felt monkey paws.

TO USE

Insert your arm into the body. Your thumb goes into the bottom of the mouth piece, your fingers at the top. The arms pass round your neck and fasten with velcro. The legs are fastened round your waist with velcro.

VENTRILOQUIST'S DUMMY

YOU WILL NEED

● balloon
● bucket
● old newspapers
● wallpaper paste
● masking tape
● cardboard toilet roll
● rubber gloves
● paint and brush
● wool for hair or an old wig if you can find one
● hat or glasses
● old sweater or shirt and tie
● needle and thread
● lots of old tights or polyester wadding for filling
● pair of old trousers
● old pair of shoes
● stick

1 Blow up the balloon and stick it in the bucket or another suitable container which will hold it whilst you are working.

2 Rip up strips of newspaper and dip them in the wallpaper paste, then cover the balloon in the strips of glue soaked paper (as for puppet p64-66).

3 Leave the papier mâché to dry and then do the next coat. When you have done three coats, then scrumple up paper to make features, nose, ears, eyes etc. Stick them into place on the balloon with the masking tape. Add more layers of papier mâché.

4 When you have done a further 2 coats of papier mâché, pop the balloon and make a hole in the neck. Insert the cardboard tube and attach it with masking tape.

Add more layers of papier mâché to secure the neck to the head.

5 Make hands by filling the rubber gloves with scrumpled newspaper and then adding layers of papier mâché round the hands and fingers.

6 Paint the head and hands a life like colour, add the features and hair, a hat and other accessories.

7 Push the neck into the clothes and sew into position. Stuff the garments with filling and then sew the hands into the ends of the sleeves and the bottom of the front of the jumper on to the trousers. Stuff the shoes into the ends of the trouser legs.

Sew together

8 Push a stick up the back of the jumper into the neck of the dummy. Use this to move its head.

Sit the dummy on your lap and start practising the techniques shown on the next page.

WORKING THE DUMMY

A ventriloquist's dummy is very difficult to use but here are a few hints.

1 Make sure the voice you give your dummy is different from your own. Pitch the voice to be higher or lower than yours or give the dummy a strong accent different from yours.

2 Relax your mouth and part your lips slightly. By working your tongue very hard you can make quite clear sounds and recognisable words without moving your lips.

3 The letters B, F, P, V and W are the most difficult to use and it might even be worth trying to write a script missing most of them out. For instance say tah-tah instead of bye bye.

4 Practise speaking for the dummy in front of a mirror.

PUSH AND PULL THEATRE

The puppets for this theatre work by being slid in and out of the box.

YOU WILL NEED

- large cardboard box
- strong all purpose adhesive
- scissors
- cardboard at least the size of one long side of the box
- 6 corks
- 2 small cup hooks
- picture frame or cardboard and gold paint or velvet
- 1cm x 1cm lengths of wood
- saw
- wood glue
- paints
- fabric for the curtains
- glue stick
- small curtain rings
- needle and thread
- 1cm ($\frac{1}{2}$ in) dowelling to support the curtain
- cardboard for figures and scenery ● brass split screws

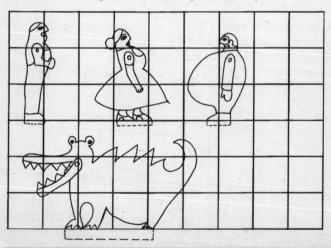

INSTRUCTIONS (for stage)

1 Cut off the flaps of the box.

2 Cut a hole in one long side of the box to make the theatre front. Leave a margin of 6cm (2½ in) all the way round.

3 Cut a hole in both short sides for the wings.

4 Cut 6cm wide strips of cardboard and stick to the stage front section to strengthen it.

5 Glue 2 corks on the inside of the box behind the upper stage front. These are for inserting the cup hooks.

6 Screw the hooks in to the corks.

7 Glue 4 more corks into position as shown on the drawing. These will hold the frame clear of the stage.

TO MAKE THE FRAME.

Either use an old picture frame of the same dimensions as the box front or cut a fancy cardboard frame and paint it gold or cover it in velvet material.

TO MAKE THE STAGE

1 Cut the 1cm x 1cm (½ in x ½ in) wood lengths to fit the width of the stage and glue them into position exactly 1cm (½ in) apart and parallel to one another.

2 Paint the wood lengths and the stage bottom white

3 Cut more 1cm x 1cm (½ in x ½ in) strips of wood to ¾ the width of the stage. The characters are glued on to the ends of these sticks and are moved by being pushed from side to side.

4 Make the curtains of lightweight fabric. Glue the seams into position and sew the rings on at regular intervals. Slip the rings on to the dowelling and then place the dowelling and curtains into position on the cup hooks.

5 Cut characters from card and paint them. Make the arms and legs jointed using brass split screws.

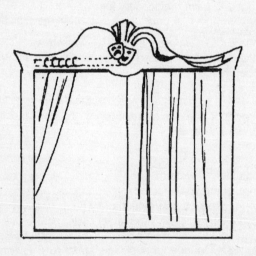

WHAT TO PERFORM

If you are going to put on a show you need a play to perform.
You can either write your own or perform someone else's
play. A good idea is to take a well-known myth or fairy tale
and make your puppets to fit in with that story.

For example, if you are going to perform Goldilocks and
the three bears you will need to make:

> Goldilocks
> father bear
> mother bear
> baby bear

You will need to paint the scenery for:

> the wood
> the kitchen (where the porridge was eaten)
> the dining room (where the chair was broken)
> the bedroom

You will need to make props:

> bowls of porridge and spoons
> three chairs
> three beds

It is a good idea to write the story as a play, marking on your
manuscript where you need scenery changes. Mark or
underline the different characters and what they say. For
example mark in red every time father bear speaks: this will
help to remind you to put on a deep voice for father bear.
Make programmes for your audience. Make sure you have
enough seats. These can of course be cushions on the floor.

You may want to put on a show to raise money for charity.
If this is so, state on the programme what you are doing and
make sure you have an official sealed collecting tin in which
to place donations.

SPECIAL EFFECTS

When you put on a show it is useful to have interesting special effects to help build up the atmosphere and make the play or show become more real. Sometimes these effects are visual and sometimes they are sounds.

RAIN: this sound is made by sprinkling uncooked rice on a baking tray. It sounds like rain on a window.

FLAMES: the sound of a fire may be made by crumpling up a ball of cellophane.

THUNDER: made by taking a large sheet of tin and shaking it violently backwards and forewards.

A CHANGE IN THE WEATHER: by using a light with a dimmer switch you can turn a sunny day into a cold wintry one.

GHOSTLY EFFECTS: coloured lightbulbs or sheets of coloured cellophane pinned on to the front of a lamp can change the whole look of the stage (but it is very important not to let the cellophane touch the bulb or you may start a fire). Reds and yellows make a warm sunny setting, blues and greens look cold and sometimes spooky.

A MARCHING ARMY: this sound is made by filling a tin with stones and shaking it up and down.

HORSE'S HOOVES: use two coconut halves or two empty paper cups and bring them alternately up and down on a table top; the faster they move the more it sounds like a galloping horse.

BIRD SONG: if you are good at whistling, do this yourself, or get a cork and wet it and then rub it over the side of a glass bottle.

If you have a tape recorder it is a good idea to go out and record the sounds you may need for a performance. For example if you wish to have vehicles, record cars, police sirens and ambulances in the street. Go to the park and record children in a playground or dogs barking or geese and ducks.

PUTTING ON A SHOW

Depending on what kind of puppets you are using you will
need a stage on which to perform your show. This can be
constructed easily and cheaply.

If you are using stick, rod or glove puppets you will work
with the puppets above your head and so you want your body
hidden from the ground upwards.

If you are using string puppets or marionettes you will
work them from above with the puppets low down. This
means you will need something to hide your body behind.

For stick or glove puppets try one of the following:

1 Place 2 chairs a metre apart and then stand them on some
large thick books. Pin an old sheet between the two chairs
and work from behind this.

2 Pin a piece ofcloth across the lower half of a door opening
and work from behind this.

3 If you are working outside pin a piece of cloth between two
trees.

4 If you can get hold of one, an old fashioned clothes horse
will make a good screen with a cloth draped over it.

PUPPET STAGE

YOU WILL NEED

- 4 thick poles or broom sticks
- 4 chairs
- some rope, string or elastic bands
- 2 sheets and drawing pins
- masking tape

INSTRUCTIONS

1 Tie the four poles to the chairs.

2 Stretch the sheet or cloth between the two chairs just above your head, and pin or tape on the two front poles.

3 Pin the other sheet between the two back poles, so that the top of the sheet is parallel with the top of the poles.

For glove puppets stand between the two sheets and work the puppets above your head (fig 1).

For string puppets, stand behind the lower sheet and bend forward with the puppets between the two sheets but showing below (fig 2).

SCENERY AND PROPS

Don't make scenery too complicated or you will not be able to see the puppets clearly.

If you have many changes of scene, paint backdrops on to sheets of paper and pin them on to the back sheet as and when you need them. For example you may wish to paint a clear sunny sky or a storm, a wild wood or a seascape or even a cosy sitting room or kitchen.

You can make bits of scenery which move. For example trees or houses can be put on sticks and moved around.

It is important to make sure props which are going to be carried are not too slippery or heavy.

HINTS ON USING PUPPETS

Glove puppets can hold and move things. For example the tug of war between Punch and Judy when they are pulling the baby back and forth between them, or the crocodile pinching sausages.

It is a good idea to store stick puppets in jars or milk bottles so they are easily to hand when you need them.

HINTS ON USING PUPPETS

Glove puppets can hold and move things. For example the tug of war between Punch and Judy when they are pulling the baby back and forth between them, or the crocodile pinching sausages.

It is a good idea to store stick puppets in jars or milk bottles so they are easily to hand when you need them.

When working glove puppets make sure you do not hold them too high or your arms will show.

Make them face one another and have one on each arm when they are talking to one another.

Get a friend to hold the puppets in position for you so you can see what they look like while they are being worked.

Check the scenery looks right before you put on your show to family and friends.

Study characters see how people and animals move and try and copy them. Old people sometimes move stiffly and slowly. A chicken will move with small jerky movements and an elephant will plod.

Watch how birds swoop and dive and dogs run and try to make your puppets look realistic.